AF270614

MIAMI DOLPHINS

KENNY ABDO

abdobooks.com

Published by Abdo Zoom, a division of ABDO, P.O. Box 398166, Minneapolis, Minnesota 55439. Copyright © 2022 by Abdo Consulting Group, Inc. International copyrights reserved in all countries. No part of this book may be reproduced in any form without written permission from the publisher. Fly!™ is a trademark and logo of Abdo Zoom.

Printed in the United States of America, North Mankato, Minnesota.
052021
092021

Photo Credits: Alamy, AP Images, Icon Sportswire, iStock, Shutterstock PREMIER
Production Contributors: Kenny Abdo, Jennie Forsberg, Grace Hansen
Design Contributors: Candice Keimig, Neil Klinepier

Library of Congress Control Number: 2020919717

Publisher's Cataloging-in-Publication Data

Names: Abdo, Kenny, author.
Title: Miami Dolphins / by Kenny Abdo
Description: Minneapolis, Minnesota : Abdo Zoom, 2022 | Series: NFL teams | Includes online resources and index.
Identifiers: ISBN 9781098224707 (lib. bdg.) | ISBN 9781098225643 (ebook) | ISBN 9781098226114 (Read-to-Me ebook)
Subjects: LCSH: Miami Dolphins (Football team)--Juvenile literature. | National Football League--Juvenile literature. | Football teams--Juvenile literature. | American football--Juvenile literature. | Professional sports--Juvenile literature.
Classification: DDC 796.33264--dc23

TABLE OF CONTENTS

MIAMI DOLPHINS

With a perfect 1972 season, two **Super Bowl** wins, and numerous division championships, the Dolphins have been hotter on the field than the Miami weather.

When asked why the Miami Dolphins were named after the aquatic mammal, team owner Joe Robbie said, "The dolphin is one of the fastest and smartest creatures in the sea."

KICK OFF

The Miami Dolphins were founded by lawyer Joe Robbie and TV star Danny Thomas in 1966. The team lost its first five games before defeating the Denver Broncos 24-7.

82

The Dolphins made it to their first **Super Bowl** following the 1971 season. But the young franchise lost to the Dallas Cowboys 24-3.

However, the 1972 season would be one for the record books. After going undefeated, the Dolphins made it back to the **Super Bowl**, beating Washington 14-7!

Miami is the only team in NFL history to have a perfect season and take home the Lombardi Trophy.

TEAM RECAPS

The Dolphins returned for **Super Bowl** VIII. This made them the first NFL team to play in the Super Bowl three years in a row. They dominated the Minnesota Vikings 24–7.

At **Super Bowl** XVII, Washington had its revenge, and beat Miami 27–17. The Dolphins made it to Super Bowl XIX, but again lost to the San Francisco 49ers 38–16.

After many disappointing seasons, the Dolphins bounced back in 2008 to win the **AFC** East. After a seven-year playoff drought, the Dolphins faced the Steelers in the wild-card round after the 2016 season. However, they'd lose 30-12.

Quarterback Ryan Tannehill and a strong defense kept Miami fans in good spirits for the 2017 season. But Tannehill suffered a season-ending knee injury in training camp. The team's record suffered, but Miami still managed to go 6–10. Miami started the 2019 season with new head coach, Brian Flores.

Kicking off the 2020 season, **rookie quarterback** Tua Tagovailoa won his first three career starts. He is the second rookie NFL quarterback since 1967 to do this without throwing an **interception**.

HALL OF FAME

Larry Little was an important part of the team's strong rushing game in the 1970s. He was a two time **Super Bowl** champion and the **AFC's** Lineman of the Year three times. Little was **inducted** into the Pro Football Hall of Fame in 1993.

Dan Marino became Miami's starting **quarterback** in 1983. The next year, he became the NFL's **MVP**. Marino is one of NFL's top ten all time passing leaders and broke many NFL passing records in his career. Marino was **inducted** into the Pro Football Hall of Fame in 2005.

Jason Taylor was a powerful defensive player for the Dolphins. During his career, he had more than 130 **sacks**. Very few NFL players have had more. In 2006, he was named the NFL's Defensive Player of the Year. Taylor was **inducted** into the Pro Football Hall of Fame in 2017.

GLOSSARY

American Football Conference (AFC) – one of two major conferences of the NFL. Each conference contains 16 teams split into four divisions. The winner of the AFC championship plays the NFC winner at the Super Bowl.

induct – to admit someone as a member of an organization.

interception – when a player catches a pass that was meant for the other team's player.

MVP – short for "most valuable player," an award given in sports to a player who has performed the best in a game or series.

quarterback (QB) – the player on the offensive team that directs teammates in their play.

rookie – a first-year player in a professional sport.

sack – when a quarterback is tackled behind the line of scrimmage while still in possession of the ball.

Super Bowl – the NFL championship game, played once a year.

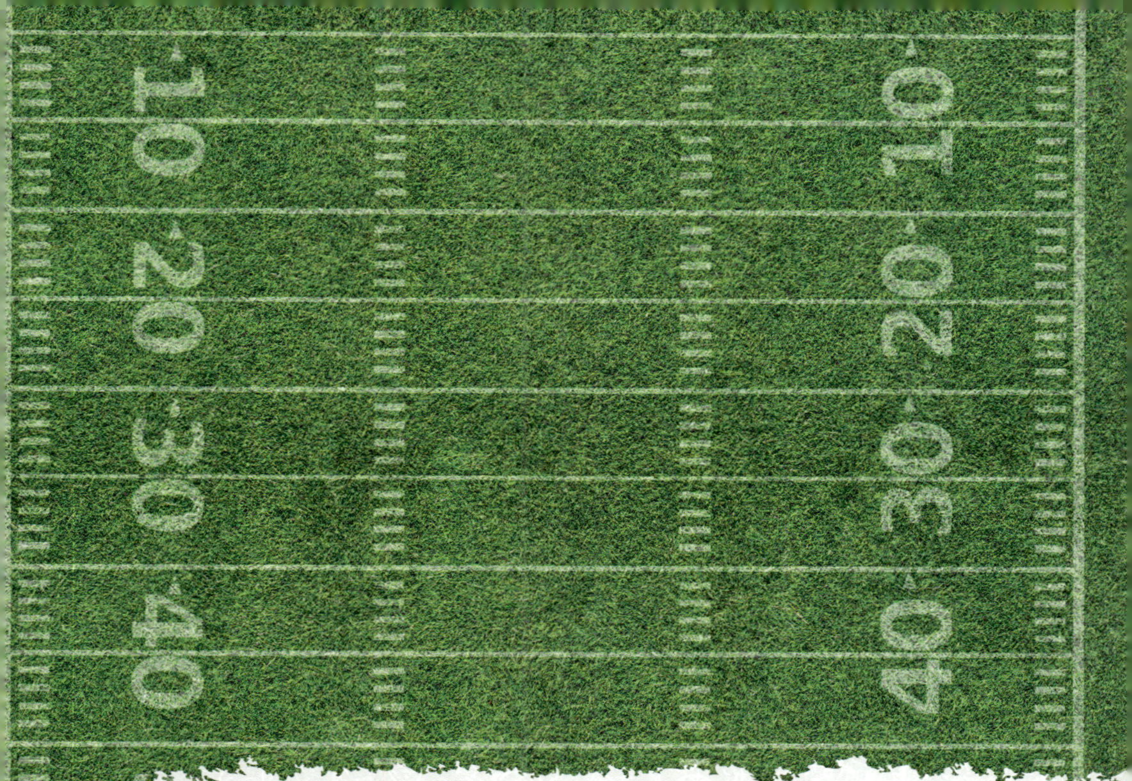

ONLINE RESOURCES

To learn more about the Miami Dolphins, please visit abdobooklinks.com or scan this QR code. These links are routinely monitored and updated to provide the most current information available.

INDEX